THE END
OF THE
COLD WAR

CHRISTINE HATT

HODDER
Wayland

an imprint of Hodder Children's Books

© 2002 White-Thomson Publishing Ltd

Produced for Hodder Wayland by
White-Thomson Publishing Ltd
2/3 St Andrew's Place
Lewes
BN7 1UP

Series concept: Alex Woolf
Editor: Joanna Bentley
Designer: Derek Lee
Consultant: Scott Lucas, Head of American and Canadian
   Studies, University of Birmingham.

Published in Great Britain in 2002 by Hodder Wayland,
a division of Hodder Children's Books

The right of Christine Hatt to be identified as the author of
this work has been asserted by her in accordance with the
Copyright, Designs and Patents Act 1988.
Illustrations by Nick Hawken.

British Library Cataloguing in Publication Data
Hatt, Christine
   The End. - (The Cold War)
   1. Cold War
   I. Title
   909.8'25

ISBN 0 7502 3393 1

Printed in Hong Kong by Wing King Tong

Hodder Children's Books
A division of Hodder Headline Limited
338 Euston Road, London NW1 3BH

Picture Acknowledgements: The publishers would like to thank
the following for giving permission to use their pictures:
Associated Press 18, 39; Camera Press *cover;* Corbis *cover;*
Corbis/© Peter Turnley 32; Polfoto 13, 33; Popperfoto
cover, 4, 6, 7, 8, 9, 11, 14, 15, 19, 24, 27 (top), 28, 29, 34,
36, 37, 40, 45, 46, 47, 49, 52, 54, 56, 57, 58; Topham
Picturepoint 12, 16, 20, 27 (bottom), 41, 42, 44, 50, 55;
United Nations 31; Wayland Picture Library 5.

Statistics source for chart on page 23:
The Military Balance 1983-1984
(The International Institute for Strategic Studies,
London, 1983)

Quotation Sources
The White House Years by Henry Kissinger (Weidenfeld &
Nicolson, 1979); *Memoirs* by Mikhail Gorbachev (Doubleday,
1996); *Jugement à Moscou. Un Dissident dans les Archives du
Kremlin* by Vladimir Boukovsky (Robert Laffont, 1995); *The
Moscow Summit, 1988: Reagan & Gorbachev in Negotiation* by
Joseph Whelan (Boulder, Westview, 1990); *At the Highest
Levels: The Inside Story of the End of the Cold War* by Michael
Beschloss and Strobe Talbott (Little Brown, 1993);
Washington Post (28 September, 1991); *The Cold War, An
International History 1947-1991* by S J Ball (Arnold/Hodder
Headline, 1998).

Contents

CHAPTER ONE

Changing Times

IN 1975 THE Cold War conflict, born 30 years earlier in the aftermath of the Second World War, started to enter a new stage. During the early 1970s, the relationship between the two superpowers at its heart – the USSR and the USA – had improved. Following a policy of détente, US President Richard Nixon and Soviet leader Leonid Brezhnev had taken important steps towards reducing tension and the possibility of nuclear war. But in mid-decade, signs of strain began to emerge.

NIXON AND KISSINGER

The state of the Cold War in 1975 was due in large part to the initiatives of US President Richard Nixon. Nixon, a Republican, had taken office in 1969. Foreign policy was his passion, and he worked to improve the USA's icy relationship with the USSR. Nixon was assisted in this challenging task by Henry Kissinger, his exceptionally able National Security Adviser, who in 1973 also became US Secretary of State.

▼ President Nixon (right) and Henry Kissinger pursued a complex foreign policy combining assertion of US strength with pursuit of détente.

PROBLEMS AND SOLUTIONS

When Nixon came to power, the USA faced two major foreign-policy problems. The first was the country's deep but increasingly unwilling involvement in the Vietnam War. Americans fighting for the non-Communist South Vietnamese against the Communist, Soviet-backed North Vietnamese were dying in their thousands. The public had long since lost its appetite for the conflict and urgently wanted the Nixon administration to end the bloodshed. The second problem was the Soviet arms build-up. In the 1960s, the USSR's stock of weapons had grown so rapidly that it now matched the American nuclear capability.

Nixon and Kissinger realized that the best way to solve both these problems was to draw closer to the USSR. The assistance of the Soviet government would be invaluable in persuading Communist North Vietnam to end the war in south-east Asia. Likewise, the USSR's co-operation would be necessary to stop the arms race spiralling out of control.

The Soviets were making similarly practical calculations. Military spending in the USSR had reached dizzying new heights, but industrial development, especially in high-technology fields such as computing, was far behind the West's. The thinking was that limited reconciliation with the USA would ease the pressure on the economy, while opening up the possibility of importing technological goods and expertise.

▲ The USA's involvement in the Vietnam War began in 1954, escalated during the 1960s and came to a bitter and unsuccessful end in 1973. The cost in human life and suffering on both sides was immense.

THE USA AND CHINA

Nixon and Kissinger adopted a twin-track approach. In November 1969, they began arms control negotiations with the USSR. These Strategic Arms Limitation Talks (SALT) proceeded at an infuriatingly slow pace. At the same time, the Americans started discussions with China, the world's other great Communist power.

The main reason for this attempt at rapprochement with China was to unsettle the Soviets. Originally staunch allies, the USSR and China had gradually fallen out over differences in policy. Throughout 1969, a violent border dispute had increased the level of hostility between them. The Soviets were wary of China's growing power, by now underpinned with nuclear weapons. So they were horrified when Nixon made an official visit to Beijing in February 1972. The prospect of an exclusive alliance between their two greatest enemies was chilling.

5

SALT I

As Nixon and Kissinger had hoped, developments in China jolted the USSR into moving forward with the SALT talks. Just three months after his visit to Beijing, the US President flew to Moscow to sign the SALT I agreement. It placed a limit of 200 anti-ballistic missiles (ABMs) on both superpowers and introduced a five-year freeze on the production of ballistic missiles.

The SALT I agreement was a landmark in Soviet-American relations. Now, after 30 years of aggression and refusal to compromise, there was an arms control foundation on which politicians could build. So, soon after, plans were made for a second round of negotiations: SALT II.

LEAVING VIETNAM

The USA's new relationship with the USSR and China helped the country to extricate itself from the war in Vietnam. Now both Communist powers put pressure on the North Vietnamese government in Hanoi to do a deal with the Americans. At the same time, the Americans stepped up their bombing campaigns, while opening secret negotiations with a senior North Vietnamese diplomat, Le Duc Tho.

Eventually, on 27 January 1973, a truce was signed, and shortly afterwards all American troops were withdrawn from Vietnam. North Vietnam went on to win the war in 1975.

THE FALL OF NIXON

By 1975, however, Richard Nixon was no longer US President. During the campaign for the 1972 presidential elections, men working for Nixon's Republican Party had bugged the offices of the opposing Democratic Party in Washington's Watergate complex. Nixon later tried to cover up this unethical activity and the resulting scandal forced him to resign in 1974.

▼ Nixon and Brezhnev (front, right) drink a toast following the signature of the SALT I agreement in Moscow on 26 May 1972.

Nixon was replaced by his Vice President, Gerald R Ford, but Henry Kissinger remained as Secretary of State. One of the new President's main foreign-policy aims was to continue détente. As a first step, he met Brezhnev in November 1974, and with him established guidelines for the planned SALT II discussions. Then, in August 1975, the two men presided over an important conference in Helsinki, Finland.

▲ Tapes recorded in President Nixon's White House office proved his full involvement in the Watergate cover-up. He chose to resign on 9 August 1974 (above), before the most incriminating tapes were released to the courts.

THE HELSINKI FINAL ACT

The Helsinki conference was attended not only by the Americans and Soviets, but also by representatives of 33 European nations. Its main purpose was finally to establish the post-1945 boundaries of Europe. In addition, delegates hoped to adopt a range of other proposals that would foster both co-operation and security in a continent now divided between Communist and democratic regimes.

The outcome of the discussions, the Helsinki Final Act, was signed on 1 August 1975. It confirmed existing European frontiers, encouraged trade and other links between European nations, and sought to guarantee human rights within Europe.

THE WAY AHEAD

Despite the upheaval caused by the fall of Nixon, the outlook for détente appeared promising in 1975. Ford and Brezhnev were both committed to the policy, if only for practical reasons, and, despite some opposition from both the public and politicians, they looked likely to prevail. In fact, the relationship between the Americans and the Soviets was about to take a turn for the worse. The Cold War had plenty of life left.

NIXON'S DÉTENTE

'An American President… has a dual responsibility: He must resist Soviet expansionism. And he must be conscious of the profound risks of global confrontation. His policy must embrace both deterrence and co-existence, both containment and an effort to relax tensions… That was what the Nixon Administration understood by détente.'

HENRY KISSINGER IN HIS BOOK *THE WHITE HOUSE YEARS*

CHAPTER TWO

The Collapse of Détente

THE ELECTION OF Democrat Jimmy Carter as US President in 1976 marked the beginning of a difficult new period in the Cold War. Over the next three years, the fragile détente built by Nixon and Ford slowly but surely collapsed. President Carter was less focused than his predecessors about his foreign-policy aims. Nevertheless, he announced two firm goals in his inaugural address: the promotion of human rights and the elimination of nuclear weapons.

▼ President Carter was inaugurated on 20 January 1977, following his election in November the previous year. After the ceremony, he, his wife Rosalynn and daughter Amy walked past the cheering crowds.

Carter's uncertain approach to foreign policy, and in particular to US-Soviet relations, was made worse by the conflict between his two main advisers. Cyrus Vance, Secretary of State from 1977, wanted to revive the détente process and to continue negotiations with the USSR so that a second SALT agreement could be quickly reached. By contrast, Zbigniew Brzezinski, Carter's National Security Adviser, wanted the USA first to establish supremacy over the USSR,

both by building up its stock of weapons, and by strengthening the North Atlantic Treaty Organization (NATO), a Western defence association set up in 1949.

Carter faced two other difficulties as he built his foreign policy. First, the public was weary of détente. Many now saw it not as a way to peace in the future but as a sign of American weakness. Second, Congress (the law-making body of the USA) was limiting presidential power over foreign policy. The 1973 War Powers Act meant that any President would have to ask Congress before sending American troops abroad. Congress also refused to lift restrictions on trade with the USSR, making it impossible to offer goods to the Soviets in exchange for compromise on political issues.

▲ Secretary of State Cyrus Vance committed himself to détente, and arms reduction talks with the USSR, as soon as he joined the Carter administration.

JIMMY CARTER (1924-)

Born in Georgia in October 1924, Jimmy Carter joined the US Navy in 1943. After his father died in the 1950s, Carter left military service to run the family peanut farms.

Carter served as a state senator from 1962 and as state governor from 1970. Voters knew him as a married man of great integrity with a deep Christian faith. He emphasized these characteristics when he ran as Democratic candidate for the presidency in 1976. They appealed to a nation recovering from the Watergate scandal, and he was duly elected.

Carter brought many skills to the White House, including high intelligence, but he found it difficult to provide strong leadership. So, although he helped to negotiate a major peace treaty between Israel and Egypt in 1979 and was an outspoken champion of human rights, his presidency is often remembered for its failures. They included failure to formulate a clear Cold War policy, to improve the ailing American economy, and to free the American hostages in Iran in 1980. Carter lost the 1980 presidential election to Republican Ronald Reagan. Since leaving office, he has worked for human rights worldwide.

RISING TENSIONS

In November 1974, President Ford had met Soviet leader Leonid Brezhnev in the Soviet port of Vladivostok to prepare a framework for SALT II. The outcome was the Vladivostok Accord, in which it was agreed that the USA and the USSR should aim to have equal numbers of nuclear missiles and missile-launchers, and at the same time work towards a steady reduction in both. This was an excellent result and rapid progress to a second treaty was therefore expected.

By March 1977, when Cyrus Vance flew to Moscow to continue discussions, the situation had changed greatly. Not only was there a new president in Washington, but Brezhnev was losing his grip. Seriously ill after a possible stroke, he could not think or speak clearly. In addition, the USA's campaign for human rights in accordance with the Helsinki Final Act, and particularly its support for dissidents and for Jews who wished to emigrate from the USSR, had angered the Soviet regime.

CYRUS ROBERTS VANCE (1917-)

President Carter's Secretary of State Cyrus Vance studied law at Yale University in Connecticut, USA. He pursued first a navy then a legal career before entering politics. Vance took up his post with the Carter administration in 1977, and for the next three years did his utmost to promote détente. However, he resigned in 1980 as a protest against the President's handling of the Iranian hostage crisis. In 1992, Vance returned to politics as United Nations negotiator at the peace talks in Bosnia-Herzegovina, a former Yugoslav republic where civil war had broken out. He retired in 1993 as a result of ill health.

The atmosphere at the negotiations soon went from bad to worse. Vance had brought with him a proposal for far greater arms reductions than those agreed at Vladivostok. The Soviets regarded this as a clumsy effort to end their superiority in intercontinental ballistic missiles (ICBMs). More generally, they deplored the Carter administration's apparent willingness to set aside the Vladivostok Accord, and took it as a clear sign that détente was no longer Washington's primary aim. So the proposal was rejected and US-Soviet relations were badly damaged as a result.

MORE MISSILES

As the political situation deteriorated, both sides started to improve the weapons available to their armed forces. In 1977, the Soviets replaced many old missiles in Eastern Europe with more accurate SS-20s. These intermediate-range weapons were designed to hit targets in Western Europe rather than the USA across the Atlantic. Western European governments were alarmed by this development. They were also angry that the USA had decided to exclude such weapons from the SALT talks.

President Carter, meanwhile, increased defence spending at home and urged his European allies in NATO to do likewise. They responded with the promise of a 3 per cent increase each year. In mid-1977, the Americans also began to develop a new type of intermediate-range cruise missile, as well as a new military aircraft, the Stealth bomber. Despite these aggressive moves, President Carter still supported the SALT talks. This dual approach owed much to the contradictory advice the President received from Brzezinski and Vance.

As cruise missiles had only an intermediate range, they had to be stationed in Europe if they were to reach the USSR. The same was true of the USA's new Pershing II ballistic missiles. So, during 1978, the Americans worked to persuade the British, West Germans, Italians, Belgians and Dutch to accept the installation of US weapons on their soil.

▼ The Soviets' intermediate-range SS-20 missiles posed a direct threat to the European members of NATO. They were also intended to warn the USA against increasing its nuclear installations on the continent.

▲ Leonid Brezhnev (left, with medals) and Jimmy Carter signed the SALT II treaty in Vienna, Austria, on 18 June 1979.

SALT II AND AFTER

Despite the setbacks that had occurred since the 1972 SALT I agreement and the 1974 Vladivostok Accord, the SALT II talks had falteringly continued. Finally, in June 1979, Carter and Brezhnev met in Vienna to sign the treaty that negotiators had prepared. Its main provisions were to restrict both sides to no more than 2,400 missiles each, and to require them to reduce that number to 2,250 by 1981. Plans were also made for a new round of arms reduction talks, SALT III, to begin.

Carter was not able to enjoy his SALT II achievement for long. Back at home, he faced serious opposition from the Senate (part of Congress), whose 100 members had to ratify the agreement before it could take effect. They were in no mood to approve what they saw as concessions to the USSR.

Nor indeed was the general public. Millions were now paying more attention to Republican Ronald Reagan, who preached hard-line resistance to the Soviet enemy.

SALT II, 1979 – THE MAIN TERMS

- Neither side to possess more than 2,400 missiles – missiles and launchers beyond the number allowed to be destroyed

- Both sides to reduce missile numbers to 2,250 by 1981

- Neither side to have more than 1,200 ICBMs (intercontinental ballistic missiles) and SLBMs (submarine-launched ballistic missiles)

- MIRVs (multiple independently targeted re-entry vehicles, that is missiles with many warheads, each directed at a different target) to have no more than ten warheads each

- Neither side permitted to make on-site inspections of the other's missiles or missile-destruction programmes

THE RETURN OF THE ARMS RACE

Zbigniew Brzezinski was pleased at this new turn of events. He realized that Jimmy Carter would now have to take a firmer stand against the Soviets if he wanted to regain the support of politicians and the public. So he urged the President to permit the development of MX missiles, which were designed to replace existing Minuteman ICBMs. Carter had little choice but to agree. The USA was already developing Trident submarines, each of which was to carry

ICBMs with nuclear warheads. Now the arms race, far from drawing to a close, was back on in earnest.

Developments in Europe added to the growing tension. Back in January 1979, due to a combination of US pressure and their own need to deter Soviet aggression against European targets, Chancellor Helmut Schmidt of West Germany and the British Prime Minister James Callaghan had finally agreed that new cruise and Pershing II ballistic missiles could be sited in their countries. There was fierce opposition among sections of the German and British populations, but not enough to alter their governments' decision. Then, at a meeting in Brussels on 12 December the same year, all NATO countries gave the go-ahead for the deployment of new US weapons in Western Europe.

ZBIGNIEW BRZEZINSKI (1928-)

Zbigniew Brzezinski was born in Poland, a country that for much of its history had suffered greatly at the hands of Russia (the dominant country in the USSR). He was educated at McGill University in Canada and Harvard University in the USA, but never forgot his Polish roots. After becoming Carter's National Security Adviser, he declared himself 'the first Pole in three hundred years in a position to really stick it to the Russians'. Accordingly, throughout his time in office he took a strong anti-détente stance. When Ronald Reagan began his first term as US President in 1981, Brzezinski left government. He then became Professor of Political Science at Columbia University, New York.

◀ People in many countries of Europe protested against the installation of American missiles on their continent. They included the Danish group Women for Peace (here collecting signatures against landmines), who supported the women's peace camp at the US air base in Greenham Common, Britain.

▲ Soviet helicopters at the airport in Kabul, the capital of Afghanistan, in January 1980. By 1985, at the height of the conflict, there were over 120,000 Red Army troops in the country.

THE INVASION OF AFGHANISTAN

The final blow to détente came from the USSR, and was prompted by events in Afghanistan, a country on its south-western border. During the 1970s, Afghanistan had become strongly pro-Soviet and had introduced many Communist policies. However, its government faced violent opposition from fundamentalist Islamic rebels, known as *mujaheddin*. The Soviets wanted to help the government resist this threat, but they were reluctant to send in troops.

The situation changed late in 1979, when a new Afghan ruler, Hafizullah Amin, seized power. Previously a firm Communist, he now began to seek Western support. The Soviet government could not permit the once-friendly regime in Afghanistan to transfer its allegiance to the USA. So, on 25 December, it sent in the Red Army to replace Amin with a Soviet-approved leader. Within five days, Amin was dead and Babrak Karmal had taken his place.

THE WEST'S RESPONSE

The West was furious at the USSR's intervention in Afghanistan. It also feared, wrongly, that this was the first stage of a Soviet plan to take over neighbouring Iran and the oil-rich Persian Gulf region. President Carter quickly punished the invaders. He withdrew SALT II from the ratification process, increased defence spending, banned grain and high technology sales to the USSR and ordered US athletes to boycott the 1980 Moscow Olympics.

The Soviets had neither wanted nor foreseen such an angry response. They had estimated that the armed intervention in Afghanistan would last only a few weeks, would end once a new leader had been imposed, and would cause little stir in the West. Instead they had locked themselves into a lengthy struggle and had done great damage to the process of détente.

President Carter summed up the USA's view of the Afghanistan invasion in early 1980. On 23 January, he used his annual State of the Union speech to declare Soviet intervention 'the most serious threat to peace since the Second World War'. He also warned the USSR that any advance into the Persian Gulf would be resisted by any means necessary, a statement that became known as the Carter Doctrine (see box). As far as the USA was concerned, détente was over and a new phase of the Cold War was about to begin.

THE CARTER DOCTRINE

'...the region now threatened by Soviet troops in Afghanistan is of great strategic importance: it contains more than two-thirds of the world's exportable oil. The Soviet effort to dominate Afghanistan has brought Soviet military forces to within 300 miles [about 483 km] of the Indian Ocean and close to the Straits of Hormuz – a waterway through which much of the free world's oil must flow. The Soviet Union is attempting to consolidate a strategic position that poses a grave threat to the free movement of Middle East oil ... let our position be absolutely clear. Any attempt by any outside force to gain control of the Persian Gulf will be regarded as an assault on the vital interests of the United States. And such an assault will be repelled by any means necessary, including military force.'

PRESIDENT JIMMY CARTER IN HIS STATE OF THE UNION SPEECH, 23 JANUARY 1980. THE FINAL TWO SENTENCES ARE KNOWN AS THE CARTER DOCTRINE.

◀ The opening ceremony of the 1980 Moscow Olympics. In protest against the Afghanistan invasion, the Games were boycotted by the USA, West Germany and several other nations. The Soviets retaliated by boycotting the 1984 Los Angeles Olympics.

Cold War II

US PRESIDENTS NIXON, Ford and Carter all opposed the Communist ideology of the USSR. However, they were also political realists, prepared to make concessions to the Soviets in order to avoid crippling the American economy and plunging the whole world into war. Carter's successor, the Republican Ronald Reagan, took a different view. To him, the struggle between the democratic USA and the Communist USSR was a struggle between good and evil, and he was ready to launch 'Cold War II' to ensure the USA won.

RONALD REAGAN

Reagan ousted Jimmy Carter in the presidential elections of November 1980. He struggled to comprehend the detail of foreign affairs, but he was absolutely certain of the broad policy that he wished to pursue in relation to the USSR. The USA was to reassert itself as the world's leading nation and to build up its military strength. Containment of Soviet power was to be the primary aim. Détente, which Carter had already sidelined following the Red Army's intervention in Afghanistan, was now completely abandoned.

▼ President Ronald Reagan during his inauguration celebrations in January 1981. Beside him is his wife, Nancy, who supported him devotedly throughout his eight years in office.

PREPARING FOR WAR

With the support of his Defense Secretary, Caspar Weinberger, Reagan launched a massive arms build-up. The plan was to increase the defence budget from $171 billion in 1981 to $367.5 billion in 1986. A new type of bomber, the B-1, was to be introduced, and the navy was to gain 144 ships, making a total of 600. The number of conventional (non-nuclear) weapons available to the American forces was to be increased, too.

THE SOVIET RESPONSE

The Soviets, who in 1981 were still under the leadership of the ailing Brezhnev, eyed these developments warily. But the poor state of the economy – by the 1980s, it was growing by 3 per cent a year, compared with 10 per cent in the 1950s – made retaliatory expansion of the Soviet defence budget a difficult option. In 1981, Brezhnev himself proclaimed to Soviet colleagues: 'we do not support the arms race, we oppose it. We could find a totally different use for the funds it swallows up.'

There was opposition to renewed military build-up for other reasons. The USSR still desperately needed Western technology, and was also dependent on grain imports to feed its people. To guarantee the continuing supply of these goods, some politicians wanted to restore, not destroy, détente. There was also a growing view that it would be impossible to 'win' a nuclear war, and that such wars were therefore best avoided altogether. Since a revived Soviet arms programme would increase tension and make conflict more likely, it was best avoided, too.

RONALD WILSON REAGAN (1911-)

Ronald Reagan was born in Tampico, Illinois. He began his working life as a sports announcer on a radio station. Then, in 1937, he moved to Hollywood, where he became an actor and appeared in over 50 films. During his Hollywood years, Reagan turned against the Democratic politics he had once supported, considering they encouraged excessive state intervention in private matters. He also gave evidence to the House Committee on Un-American Activities, a government body that set out to discover and denounce Communists. Finally, in 1962, he joined the Republican Party.

Reagan served as Governor of California from 1967 to 1975, where his political skills and easy charm won him many admirers. He failed to gain the Republican presidential nomination in 1968 or 1976, but won the presidency itself in 1980 and 1984. In office, he cut welfare schemes and taxes at home, while pursuing an aggressive anti-Communist foreign policy abroad. His negotiations with Soviet leader Mikhail Gorbachev played a major part in ending the Cold War. Reagan left government in 1989 and was replaced by his Vice President, George Bush.

PROBLEMS IN POLAND

Since the Second World War, there had been Communist governments right across Eastern Europe and most had been firmly under Soviet control. However in the 1980s, the USSR started to lose its influence. The trouble began in Poland, where the people's resistance increased after the 1979 visit of new Polish Pope John Paul II.

SHORTAGES AND STRIKES

Following President Carter's suspension of détente, the USA cut back exports to the USSR and its Eastern European satellites severely. Poland had long suffered from shortages of food, consumer goods and high technology, so was hit especially hard. When the government of Edward Gierek made matters worse by doubling meat prices in July 1980, Poles rose up in protest and strikes spread across the country. A poor harvest later that year only fuelled the tensions.

▼ Solidarity leader Lech Walesa (below right) with Poland's Deputy Prime Minister Mieczyslaw Jagielski in August 1980. The Polish government's recognition of Solidarity and acceptance of its early demands were not enough to prevent further unrest.

THE BIRTH OF SOLIDARITY

A major centre of unrest was the Lenin shipyard in Gdansk on the Baltic coast, where a strike began in mid-August. The government started pay negotiations there, as elsewhere, in an attempt to persuade people back to work. But they could not damp down the new mood of enthusiasm for change. During the same month, thousands of Gdansk workers, led by a charismatic unemployed electrician called Lech Walesa, set up a trade union. It was known as Solidarnosc, Polish for 'Solidarity'.

The Soviet leadership was infuriated when the Polish government recognized the new union, but decided not to send in troops immediately. Instead they ordered the regime to do everything in its power to defeat the Solidarity movement. Soon afterwards, Gierek was replaced by a more robust leader, Stanislaw Kania. The Americans, meanwhile, were secretly supporting Walesa and his followers.

A GROWING MOVEMENT

The Soviets' non-military approach did not work. Soon Solidarity had some 10 million members and their demands grew daily. Economic improvements such as better pay were no longer enough. Now they were determined to achieve political change too.

These developments led to mounting alarm in Moscow. Brezhnev and his colleagues knew they needed to act decisively and began to draw up plans for military intervention. However, they also knew Solidarity was supported by Western democracies and the Roman Catholic Church. Violent repression of the union was likely to provoke international condemnation and escalation of the Cold War.

▲ A stern-faced General Wojciech Jaruzelski declares martial law in 1981.

MARTIAL LAW

In the event, the government in Poland solved its own problems. On 9 February 1981, former Defence Minister General Wojciech Jaruzelski took over as Prime Minister. The Soviets were content to work through this hard-line Communist and encouraged him to neutralize Solidarity by whatever means necessary.

Solidarity, however, continued to gain support. By late 1981, Poland was descending into chaos as strikes and anti-Communist protests flared up right across the country. Eventually, on 13 December 1981, Jaruzelski declared martial law.

Events then began to move fast. Solidarity was banned, Lech Walesa was arrested, and troops were sent on to the streets to restore order. The Soviet leadership had got their way. But the Poles now knew their own power, and soon they and many other Eastern Europeans began to fight back.

POLAND'S UPRISING

'...the working men and women of Poland have set an example for all those who cherish freedom and dignity.'

PRESIDENT JIMMY CARTER, SEPTEMBER 1980

'Solidarity has been transformed into an organised political force, which is able to paralyse the activity of the party and state organs and take de facto power into its own hands. If [Solidarity] has not yet done that, then it is primarily because of its fear that Soviet troops would be introduced and because of its hopes that it can achieve its aims without bloodshed and by means of a creeping counter-revolution.'

THE SOVIET POLITBURO, APRIL 1981

SALT, START AND INF

The US Congress never ratified the SALT II treaty. However, in May 1982 President Reagan promised that if the USSR did not break the agreement, nor would the USA. At the same time, at the request of Congress, he proposed a new round of SALT negotiations, to be renamed START (Strategic Arms Reduction Talks) and held in Geneva. The prospects were not good, as the USA was unwilling to cut back any of its main long-range systems, such as the MX ICBMs.

INF

Running alongside the START negotiations in Switzerland were Intermediate-Range Nuclear Forces (INF) talks. They were intended to deal with nuclear missiles sited in Europe that could travel only far enough to hit targets in Europe (including the western, European regions of Russia). The new

▼ At Brezhnev's funeral in November 1982, the leading members of the Soviet Communist Party carried him in an open casket. The man at the front wearing glasses is Brezhnev's successor, Yuri Andropov.

cruise and Pershing II missiles, which had yet to be deployed, numbered among these weapons.

There was much debate between members of the Reagan administration, including Defense Secretary Caspar Weinberger and new Secretary of State George Shultz, about exactly what these talks should try to achieve. As many Europeans did not want the new missiles on their soil, the USA proposed a 'zero option'. It involved offering to deploy none of the weapons in return for the Soviets removing all SS-4, SS-5 and SS-20 missiles from Europe. At the time the USSR was not prepared to give up so much, so no real progress was made and the talks stumbled on into 1983.

BREZHNEV AND ANDROPOV

In November 1982 Leonid Brezhnev died and was quickly replaced as Communist Party General Secretary by Yuri Andropov. Another old, sick man, Andropov now took charge of a country with a crumbling economy but massive military commitments.

Andropov's main aim was to improve the Soviet economy in order to strengthen the USSR's international position. He also set out to renew détente by making several proposals, including an offer to reduce SS-20 missile numbers in Europe. At the same time, he fervently hoped that European peace protesters would persuade the USA not to deploy new weapons.

LEONID ILYICH BREZHNEV (1906-1982)

Brezhnev came from the Ukraine, then a south-western region of the USSR, and joined the Communist Party as a young man. He rose gradually through the party ranks until 1952, when his skills were noticed by Soviet leader Josef Stalin. He was then quickly brought into the Politburo, the government's main policy-making body. On Stalin's death in 1953, Brezhnev lost his post in Moscow, but was restored to a position of power by new leader Nikita Khrushchev, whom he had known in the Ukraine. After Khrushchev was ousted in 1964, Brezhnev took over as Communist Party General Secretary.

A dull, uninspiring man, Brezhnev nevertheless introduced a dynamic foreign policy based on increasing Soviet military spending and influence abroad. In 1968, when the Red Army invaded Czechoslovakia to stop the government relaxing Communist rule, he also formulated the Brezhnev Doctrine. It proclaimed that the USSR had the right to enforce the Soviet-approved form of Communism in the states under its control.

Brezhnev became seriously ill in 1976 – he had probably suffered a stroke. The rest of the government hid his condition, however, and ruled on his behalf, taking the decision to invade Afghanistan in 1979. After struggling on for six years, Brezhnev died in 1982, aged 75.

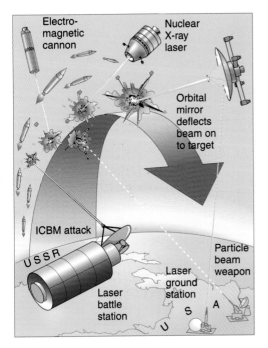

Electro-
magnetic
cannon

Nuclear
X-ray
laser

Orbital
mirror
deflects
beam on
to target

ICBM attack

USSR

Laser
battle
station

Laser
ground
station

Particle
beam
weapon

USA

▲ This diagram is an artist's
impression of the planned
SDI system. It shows how
particle beams, lasers and
electromagnetic cannon would
work together to destroy
incoming Soviet missiles.

STAR WARS

In spring 1983, as Yuri Andropov was attempting to put his country's relationship with the USA on a more friendly footing, President Ronald Reagan denounced the USSR as an 'evil empire'. He then launched the Strategic Defense Initiative (SDI), a high-technology programme designed to protect the USA from incoming enemy missiles. To the general public, it sounded like something from science-fiction, so instantly became known as Star Wars.

A PERFECT PLAN?

At first hearing, the theory of SDI sounded perfect. An electronic shield would be erected in space around the USA so that nothing could break through. At the same time, lasers and particle beams would shoot down any weapons that tried. It did not take long, however, for the flaws to become apparent. The most obvious were that no one knew whether the initiative would work or how much it would cost.

There were other major problems. SDI would totally disrupt the balance of power that had for almost 40 years stopped the Cold War turning violent. Each side had known that if it launched a nuclear attack, the other had the ability to respond with equal force. This knowledge had acted as a highly effective deterrent. But if the new system worked, the USA would be invulnerable. The Soviets responded to this alarming prospect by declaring that they would develop missiles capable of penetrating the SDI shield.

Western Europeans, the USA's partners in democracy, were far from content either. SDI would offer them no protection whatsoever. On the contrary, it would make them the only realistic targets for Soviet aggression. But Ronald Reagan, SDI's most ardent devotee, was determined to go ahead. Despite some resistance, he soon secured $14.68 billion funding from Congress.

FLIGHT KAL 007

As 1983 continued, the superpower relationship rapidly went from bad to worse. One particular incident symbolized the deteriorating situation. On the last day of August, Flight KAL 007, a Korean Airlines passenger jet travelling from Alaska to Seoul, left its proper course and flew into Soviet airspace. Apparently fearing the presence of a spy plane, Soviet fighters shot down the jet, causing the deaths of all 269 people on board.

The tragedy provoked an international chorus of outrage, led by the USA. The Soviets' clumsy and unconvincing efforts to defend themselves only made matters worse. Experts are still unsure why KAL 007 was flying so far from its normal path. Whatever the truth, at the time the USA saw the episode as indisputable proof of Soviet barbarity.

START STOPS

1983 drew to its close with another setback. In November, the Pershing II ballistic missiles and ground-launched cruise missiles were deployed in Great Britain and West Germany. The Soviets considered this a sign that the Americans had no real commitment to the START and INF talks in Geneva. Accordingly, their negotiators walked out.

MILITARY POWER: UNITED STATES vs USSR, 1983-1984

	USA	USSR
Intercontinental Ballistic Missiles	1,045	1,398
Submarine-launched Ballistic Missiles	568	980
Long-range Strategic Bombers	272	143
Total Delivery Vehicles (ICBMs, SLBMs, Bombers)	1,885	2,521
Nuclear Warheads (ICBMs and SLBMs)	7,297	8,343
Destructive Power (in millions of tonnes of TNT)	2,202	5,111
Anti-ballistic Missile Launchers (ABM)	0	32
Aircraft Carriers	14	5
Armed Forces Personnel	2,136,400	5,050,000

SIGNS OF HOPE

In 1984 Ronald Reagan, hoping to avoid conflict during an election year, began to soften the tone of his remarks about the USSR, and to speak openly of the need for more arms control.

In the USSR, Andropov's brief term of office ended with his death on 9 February. His replacement by another elderly politician, Konstantin Chernenko, promised little change in Soviet attitudes. In fact, the new leader was so ill with emphysema that his spell in power was to be even shorter than Andropov's. But meanwhile, paralysing distrust of the Americans continued to make real progress difficult.

▼ President Reagan's Secretary of State George Shultz (left) and Soviet Foreign Minister Andrei Gromyko meet in Geneva in January 1985. While Shultz smiles for the cameras, Gromyko's wariness is obvious.

REVIVING THE ARMS TALKS

Back in January, as part of his new approach to the USSR, Reagan had sent his Secretary of State, George Shultz, to meet Soviet Foreign Minister Andrei Gromyko. Their discussions had been both lengthy and constructive. At a United Nations meeting in November, the President had talks with Gromyko himself, and was favourably impressed. So, when he was re-elected soon afterwards, he arranged for Shultz and Gromyko to meet again in January 1985. The hope was that they could revive the arms control talks that had ended so disastrously late in 1983.

A LEADER IN WAITING?

While Chernenko lived out his last months as Soviet leader, younger men were preparing to introduce new ways of approaching the old Cold War problems. Among them was Mikhail Gorbachev, already a high-flying Politburo member. In December 1984, he visited London to meet the British Prime Minister, Margaret Thatcher. A loyal supporter of President Reagan and his anti-Communist stance, she was nevertheless enchanted by this dynamic man, who looked like a leader in waiting.

REAGAN IN CHINA

There was change in Communist China, too. Since Nixon's 1972 visit to the country, its friendship with the USA had become no closer than exchanging ambassadors in 1979. This was partly because Americans had continued selling arms to its Nationalist Chinese enemies on the island of Taiwan, hoping they might one day return to power on the mainland. But by the 1980s, even President Reagan had accepted that the Communists were in control of China for good. So although the USA no longer needed China as an ally in its Cold War struggle against the USSR, the President visited the country in April 1984.

WINNING FRIENDS

'I like Mr Gorbachev. We can do business together.'

BRITISH PRIME MINISTER MARGARET THATCHER, DECEMBER 1984.

CHAPTER FOUR

The War Around The World

THE MAIN BATTLEGROUNDS of the Cold War were the USA, the USSR and Europe. However, the American and Soviet regimes both saw their ideological conflict as a global struggle. As a result, they were ready to intervene anywhere in the world to support their cause. During Cold War II (1979-1985), such intervention occurred in many developing countries and served to worsen tensions between the two main players.

EL SALVADOR

The Reagan administration did not confine its intervention in Central America to Nicaragua. In 1979, the Farabundo Marti National Liberation Front (FMLN), a left-wing guerrilla group, had challenged El Salvador's ruling right-wing party. However, it failed to win power and a civilian-military junta seized control. Under its rule, human rights abuses became common. In 1980 Oscar Romero, Archbishop of the country's capital, San Salvador, was assassinated. Soon after, three American nuns were also killed and President Carter suspended US aid. He restored it in early 1981, however, when the FMLN launched an attack on the junta.

During Reagan's time in office, aid to the junta was increased from $36 million in 1981 to $197 million in 1984. Reagan considered that José Napoleon Duarte, El Salvador's President for much of the 1980s, was a sufficiently moderate figure to support against the left-wing FMLN. This was despite the fact that, under Duarte's rule, the junta sent out military 'death squads' that killed about 40,000 civilians.

TROUBLE IN NICARAGUA

The USA had always been anxious to stop Communism taking hold in Central America, its own 'backyard'. In order to do so, it had even been content to support ruthless right-wing dictators with little regard for their people's human rights. Such was the case in Nicaragua, where the rich Somoza family had ruled since 1936. In 1979, however, the left-wing Sandinista rebels finally managed to overthrow General Anastasio Somoza and to establish a government led by Daniel Ortega Saavedra.

President Carter responded with caution. He did not care for the new government, but still sent financial aid. This seemed a wiser option than forcing the Sandinistas to turn to the USSR or the Communist regime in nearby Cuba for help. Carter reduced the assistance before leaving office, then President Reagan stopped it completely in 1981. As a result the Cubans, in fact already involved in Nicaragua, began to play a larger role, providing the regime with doctors and other experts.

SUPPORTING THE CONTRAS

The Americans were not the only people to dislike the Sandinistas. Many middle-class Nicaraguans who had lost power and property under their rule also opposed them. They backed an armed group known as the Contras, who in 1981 began a civil war designed to throw out Ortega and his government. By November, the Reagan administration was supporting the Contras with money, arms and military training.

In 1983, however, Reagan's anti-Communist operation began to fall apart. When he asked Congress to approve funds for the continuing struggle against the Sandinistas, its members turned him down. Then, a year later, they passed the Boland Amendment. It stated baldly that no further government money was to be spent in Central America.

THE IRAN-CONTRA AFFAIR

Reagan was not prepared to let the matter rest, so looked for ways of backing the Contras by stealth. This led to the creation of a complex and illegal funding arrangement. In the 1980s, the USA began to supply Iran with arms in return for hostages. Then a marine officer, Lieutenant Colonel Oliver North, had the idea of using profits from the arms sales to fund the Contras. It is unclear whether Reagan knew what North was doing. But when the scheme was discovered in November 1986, the public's faith in Reagan was severely shaken.

GRENADA

President Reagan's third intervention in the Americas was in the small Caribbean island of Grenada. In October 1983, its government was overthrown by left-wing activists, which provoked Reagan to send in 1,900 troops.

After the invasion, a non-political council was appointed to rule, and Reagan proclaimed that the USA had prevented Grenada from becoming a Soviet-Cuban colony.

▼ Oliver North, the man who implemented the illegal Contras funding scheme. When he appeared before a 1987 Congressional hearing, North argued that his conduct was a justifiable way of counteracting Communism.

THE COLD WAR IN AFRICA

By the early twentieth century, Africa had become a patchwork of European colonies. But from the 1950s, one after another won its independence. Many of the new countries that emerged were deeply divided, with opposing factions prepared to use violence to gain control. The USA and USSR soon imported the Cold War conflict into these battle zones. Each was determined to ensure its ideology held sway across the continent.

UNREST IN ANGOLA

The country of Angola in south-west Africa had become a Portuguese colony in the fifteenth century. From the mid-twentieth century, three guerrilla groups led its struggle for independence. Each had different political ideas and members of different tribes. The Movement for the Liberation of Angola (MPLA) was Communist and had leaders of mixed race. The National Front for the Liberation of Angola (FNLA) was anti-Communist and supported by the Bakongo tribe. The political allegiance of the National Union for the Total Independence of Angola (UNITA) was less clear-cut, but most members belonged to the Ovimbundu tribe.

▼ In this 1976 scene from the Angolan civil war, American-backed UNITA soldiers inspect a railway bridge across the River Lumege that Soviet-backed MPLA forces have all but destroyed.

SUPERPOWER INVOLVEMENT

Angola was a prize for which both the USA and the USSR were ready to fight. Their incentives were largely political, but they were also keen to acquire an interest in the country's oil, gas and diamond reserves. Each of the two powers backed the guerrilla force that most closely shared its ideology, the Soviets supporting the MPLA, the Americans the FNLA. Other nations became involved, too. The Cubans, for example, provided the MPLA with military training, while the Chinese backed the FNLA in an effort to stop their Soviet enemies gaining influence in the region.

INDEPENDENCE AND AFTER

The situation worsened after April 1974, when the dictator of Portugal, Antonio Salazar, was ousted. In January 1975, it was announced that Angola would be granted independence in November. At first, the guerrilla groups seemed ready to work together. But then the superpowers increased military and financial aid, fuelling unrest.

Other factors contributed to the rising violence. In mid-1975, the USA began to fund UNITA as well as FNLA, and anti-Communist South Africa sent troops to fight alongside UNITA too. Cuba and the USSR responded by massively increasing military support for the MPLA. But the Ford administration, denied more funds by Congress, could do nothing else to help its allies.

THE PEOPLE'S REPUBLIC

The Congress decision, coupled with South Africa's withdrawal, ensured MPLA victory. In 1976, it set up the People's Republic of Angola, based in Luanda, and signed a friendship treaty with the USSR. FNLA/UNITA meanwhile set up the People's Democratic Republic of Angola in Huambo, but it won little international recognition. The USA had demonstrably lost this Cold War battle. But when fighting in Angola restarted, it continued secretly to support the anti-MPLA rebels.

▼ In 1977, troops from Somalia in north-east Africa invaded neighbouring Ethiopia's Ogaden desert. With Soviet help, the Ethiopians forced them out the following year. This photograph shows young Somali troops in a training camp on captured Ethiopian land.

IRAN

The USA suffered a major loss of influence in one part of the Middle East during the 1970s. Iran, an important provider of oil to the West, had long been a close ally. However its ruler, Shah Mohammed Reza Pahlavi, was growing unpopular because of his rapid Westernization of Iranian society – many fundamentalist Muslims in the country wanted instead to preserve traditional values.

In 1978, rioting finally broke out, and in January 1979 the shah fled Iran. Soon after, Ayatollah Ruholla Khomeini, a Muslim cleric who had been living in exile, returned to the country. He then set up an Islamic government that was deeply hostile to the Americans. Tension rose in October, when the shah entered the USA for medical treatment. In protest, students took over the US embassy in Teheran, the Iranian capital, on 4 November. Fifty-eight Americans were taken hostage.

President Carter did not handle the crisis well. First he made several unsuccessful attempts to negotiate the hostages' release. Then, wrongly fearing the Soviets were about to intervene, he warned them off with the Carter Doctrine. Finally, in April 1980, he authorized a helicopter rescue mission to Teheran. Its humiliating failure was partly responsible for his defeat in the 1980 presidential election. The hostages were finally released in January 1981, as Ronald Reagan took office.

THE COLD WAR IN THE MIDDLE EAST

From early in the Cold War, the USA was determined to prevent Soviet influence in the Middle East. The reason was simple: more than 60 per cent of the West's oil supplies came from that area. The USSR, however, was as eager to promote Communism there as anywhere else. This superpower rivalry soon began to fuel the existing hostility between the peoples of the region. Since the establishment of Israel in 1948, the state's Jews had regularly and violently clashed with the surrounding Arab majority.

TAKING SIDES

During the 1960s, the Soviets supplied several Arab states with weapons and supported them in disputes with Israel. By contrast the USA, encouraged by a strong Jewish lobby at home, often took the Israeli side. This division of interests became more severe after the Six Day War of 1967, during which the Israelis dramatically defeated Egypt, Jordan and Syria. Afterwards, the Soviets supplied Egypt with new military equipment and established bases there.

The situation changed in 1972, when Egyptian president Anwar Sadat fell out with the Soviets, claiming they were more interested in concluding the SALT I talks with the USA than helping Egypt recover land lost in the Six Day War. In protest, he expelled all Soviet military experts from his country. A year later, in October 1973, Egypt and Syria launched a surprise attack on Israel during the Jewish religious holiday of

Yom Kippur. As usual, the USSR sided with the Arabs and the USA with the Israelis. Tensions ran high – at one stage the USA was on nuclear alert – but a ceasefire was finally introduced.

CAMP DAVID AND AFTER

From 1973, US Secretary of State Henry Kissinger played a central role in promoting Middle East peace. Flying regularly between Egypt, Syria and Israel, he slowly drew the opposing sides closer together. The Soviets were excluded from all talks in order to highlight their loss of influence in the region.

The prospects for peace increased in 1977, when President Sadat visited Israel. The following year, he and the Israeli Prime Minister, Menachem Begin, joined President Carter for talks at his Camp David retreat. This led to the Camp David Accords, which outlined frameworks for future negotiations. A peace treaty between Egypt and Israel was finally signed in 1979. Under its terms the Sinai Peninsula, seized by Israel during the Six Day War, was returned.

The 1979 treaty was an important but limited document. In particular, it failed to solve the problem of the West Bank, another territory won by the Israelis in 1967, but which was home to thousands of Palestinians. Many Arab states refused to accept the treaty. So did the USSR, thus ensuring the Cold War divide in the Middle East was as wide, and as dangerous, as it had ever been.

▲ Egyptian President Anwar Sadat (left), US President Jimmy Carter and Israeli Prime Minister Menachem Begin (right) clasp hands in friendship after their Camp David meetings of September 1978.

LEBANON

Lebanon, to the north of Israel, was another country where the USA and USSR clashed. The nation was divided on many levels, most notably between Christians and Muslims, who began a civil war in 1975. It was also home to thousands of Palestinians who had fled their homeland after the foundation of Israel. Many belonged to the Palestine Liberation Organization (PLO), which launched regular rocket attacks on the Israelis across the border.

In 1982, Israel invaded Lebanon to punish the PLO. The Israelis fought with American arms, while the Syrians defended the Palestinians using Soviet weapons. American marines were then sent to Lebanon as part of a UN peace-keeping force. They soon became involved in the civil war and provoked Muslim hostility. President Reagan turned down Congress requests to pull them out, claiming they were protecting the country from Soviet influence. But in 1983, after a Muslim terrorist drove an explosive-packed truck into an American barracks, killing 239 men, he issued the order to withdraw. All troops had left by early 1984.

31

CHAPTER FIVE

The New Political Thinking

KONSTANTIN CHERNENKO DIED on 10 March 1985, after little more than a year in office. The next day he was replaced as General Secretary of the Soviet Communist Party by Mikhail Gorbachev. Gorbachev's *novoye myshlenniye* (new political thinking) would transform both his own country and its relations with the West in just a few eventful years.

THE SOVIET ECONOMY

Even before he came to power, Gorbachev had taken a long, hard look at the creaking Soviet economy. Military spending swallowed up about half the USSR's gross national product. The provision of aid to Cuba, Afghanistan and other Communist allies was a further drain on resources, costing up to $40 billion per year. At home, tight central government control over industry had stifled initiative, leading to low output. Every citizen felt the effects of this economic mismanagement. Wages and living standards were low, and housing was poor.

▼ During the Soviet era, food shortages were common across the USSR, and people had to queue even for basic goods such as bread.

TIME FOR REFORM

Gorbachev realized that the only way to avoid economic disaster was to introduce radical reforms. They were to have two main themes. The first was *perestroika*: restructuring of the economy. The second was *glasnost*: increased openness in politics. It was obvious that it would be impossible to restructure the economy without cutting military spending. So Gorbachev set out to do business with the Americans.

A NEW START

Soviet Foreign Minister Andrei Gromyko and US Secretary of State George Shultz had already met in January 1985. At talks in Geneva, the two men had agreed to revive the START and INF talks, as well as to begin discussions about defence systems such as SDI. After some months, it was also agreed that Gorbachev and Reagan should hold a summit conference in November.

During the summer and autumn of 1985, Gorbachev prepared for the summit. In July, he replaced the dour Foreign Minister Andrei Gromyko with the more charismatic Eduard Shevardnadze, who shared Gorbachev's total commitment to change. Then with Shevardnadze, he formulated his new approach to relations with the Western democracies.

This approach had several beliefs at its core. First, superpower rivalry was not only damaging but pointless. The arms race could never be won, but would continue endlessly as first one power then the other edged ahead. Second, superpower backing for military conflict in developing countries had achieved little at great cost. Joint humanitarian aid would be a far better option. Third, and following on from the first two beliefs, lasting peace and security could be achieved only through politics.

Gorbachev also intended that, under his guidance, the Soviet government would show greater concern for freedom of speech and other human rights. He believed this development would ease relations with the West, which had long criticized the USSR's harsh repression of dissent.

▲ Soviet Foreign Minister Eduard Shevardnadze (left) meets his Danish counterpart Uffe Ellemann Jensen in September 1988.

MAKING PROGRESS

In this extract from his Memoirs (1996), Gorbachev explains the reasoning behind the new Soviet approach to the West.

'We [the Soviet leadership] understand that in today's world of mutual interdependence, progress is unthinkable for any society which is fenced off from the world by impenetrable state frontiers and ideological barriers. A country can develop its full potential by interacting with other societies, yet without giving up its own identity.

We realised that we could not ensure our country's security without reckoning with the interests of other countries, and that, in our nuclear age, you could not build a safe security system based solely on military means. This prompted us to propose an entirely new concept of global security, which included all aspects of international relations, including the human dimension.'

THE GENEVA SUMMIT

Reagan and Gorbachev were very different people. The US President, an actor by training, had come to politics late in life. By the time of the Geneva summit he was 74, and his grasp of policy detail, never strong, was fading. The Soviet leader, by contrast, was a 54-year-old career politician at the height of his powers. This mismatch promised to make negotiations difficult, but in fact a strong rapport developed between the two men. It played no small part in bringing the Cold War to an end.

SETTING THE SCENE

Both the USA and the USSR began preparing their negotiating positions weeks in advance of the summit. The Soviets, who for economic reasons needed progress on arms control more urgently than the Americans, offered some important concessions. They included reduction of SS-20 numbers in Europe from 270 to 243, and a halving of strategic (long-range) warheads. The Americans were also ready, in principle, to cut back on intermediate and strategic weapons. SDI, however, was not up for discussion. If the Soviets did not approve, that was just too bad.

SUMMIT SUCCESS

Reagan and Gorbachev met in Geneva on 19 November 1985. Their first talk, scheduled to last just 15 minutes, continued for an hour. It was not a friendly occasion, however, as each man took the chance to make forthright criticisms of

▼ Mikhail Gorbachev (left) and Ronald Reagan laugh and shake hands at the end of the Geneva summit on 21 November 1985. Both men had good cause to be relieved and happy at the outcome of the talks.

the other's political ideology and foreign policy. At a second meeting later in the day, the inevitable clash over SDI occurred. Then, after a walk outside in the crisp Geneva air, the two leaders returned to their villa for a 'fireside chat'. It was a turning point – they started to relax and simply get along.

The summit continued for another day, with Reagan and Gorbachev talking amicably about the broad outline of policy while their negotiating teams dealt with the detail. By the end, the participants were able to issue a joint communiqué. It stated that they would work to prevent war between them, nuclear or conventional, and would begin new arms control talks. These would aim to reduce both sides' nuclear capability by 50 per cent – the race for military superiority was off the agenda. The Soviets also pledged to withdraw all their troops from Afghanistan as soon as politically and practically possible.

A NEW RELATIONSHIP

The 1985 Geneva summit led to no binding agreements, except on a few scientific and cultural matters. But it altered the superpower relationship on both a personal and a political level. Now the two men at the top really wanted to make it work, and with their teams they had committed themselves to a programme of action. Of course, there were still massive obstacles in the way of progress, not least the deadlock over SDI, but it seemed a way to overcome them might one day be found.

MIKHAIL SERGEYEVICH GORBACHEV (1931-)

Mikhail Gorbachev was born in Privolnoye in the south-western Caucasus region of Russia. He studied law at Moscow University, and after graduating he returned to the Caucasus, where he worked for Komsomol, the Communist Youth League, then rose to become local party chief. In 1978, the Soviet leadership called Gorbachev to Moscow to take the post of agriculture secretary in the Communist Party Central Committee. In 1979 he joined the Politburo, then in 1985, following Konstantin Chernenko's death, became Communist Party General Secretary.

In his new role, Gorbachev revitalized Soviet foreign policy, while introducing major reforms at home. His main economic goals were to replace the centrally planned Soviet economy with a semi-market economy and to modernize industry and agriculture. Politically, he set out to restructure the Communist Party, to purge it of corruption, and to organize more democratic elections for officials. He also permitted moves towards multiparty democracy. In 1990, he was appointed to the new, American-style role of President. In the same year, he won the Nobel Prize for Peace.

Despite his efforts, in August 1991, Gorbachev was ousted in a hard-line Communist coup and, after a brief return to power, he resigned on 25 December. He now devotes much of his time to the Gorbachev Foundation, which raises funds for people in need, including victims of the Chernobyl explosion.

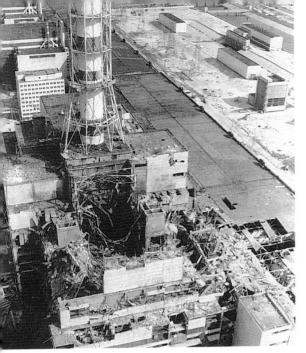

▲ An aerial view of the Chernobyl nuclear power station, showing the extent of the destruction that the 1986 explosion caused.

DISASTER IN CHERNOBYL

On 26 April 1986, staff carrying out tests at a nuclear power station in Chernobyl, Ukraine, failed to follow the correct safety procedures. As a result, the reactor exploded and caught fire, sending clouds of radioactive dust into the atmosphere. The wind soon carried them far and wide, with the result that much of Europe was affected.

The incident highlighted the economic and political problems of the USSR. The Chernobyl reactor was out of date, badly designed and poorly maintained, while the authorities were slow to respond to the explosion and did their best to conceal its enormity from the outside world. Gorbachev later said that the disaster was a turning point for *glasnost*. It showed beyond any doubt that the secretive, lumbering style of Soviet government was long overdue for reform.

SOVIET INITIATIVES

For Gorbachev, 1986 began with a flurry of activity. In January, he made an ambitious new proposal: the USSR would aim to eliminate all nuclear weapons by 2000. He also presented a plan for the withdrawal of all Soviet and US intermediate-range forces from Europe.

The USA thought Gorbachev's arms reduction plan was literally too good to be true. It also failed to address the fact that the USSR had far more conventional forces in Europe than the USA, so if all superpower nuclear missiles were removed, the Western nations would be at a disadvantage. To the annoyance of his own military, the Soviet leader had offered to redeploy some troops elsewhere. But this was not enough for the USA, who knew Soviet forces would still outnumber the West's.

RISING TENSIONS

The Soviets were disappointed at the Americans' lack of enthusiasm for their proposals. Two further developments made them angry, too. The first was the USA's decision to increase aid and supply Stinger anti-aircraft missiles to Afghanistan's *mujaheddin*. By the autumn, the Islamic rebels were using these new weapons to shoot down Soviet helicopters. The second occurred on 15 April, when US aircraft bombed Libya, a Soviet ally, believing it was responsible for a Berlin night-club bombing that had killed a US soldier.

THE REYKJAVIK SUMMIT

Despite these and other problems – both the USA and USSR arrested alleged spies in August – Gorbachev continued to push for another summit. Eventually, it was agreed that he and Reagan would meet again on 11 October in Reykjavik, Iceland. The talks there made rapid progress. Both sides quickly accepted the 'zero option' proposal to withdraw all intermediate-range weapons. Then, after hours of debate, the two leaders took the amazing step of agreeing to eliminate all nuclear weapons in a decade.

It was not to be. Gorbachev insisted he would confirm the new arms reduction plan only if the Americans confined SDI research to the laboratory. Reagan was adamant he would never agree to such a request. For the sake of Star Wars, the huge gains of the summit were thrown away.

VIEWS OF REYKJAVIK

'Believe me, the significance of that meeting at Reykjavik is not that we didn't sign agreements in the end; the significance is that we got as close as we did. The progress we made would've been inconceivable just a few months ago.'

PRESIDENT REAGAN TALKING TO REPORTERS ABOUT THE OUTCOME OF THE REYKJAVIK SUMMIT, 14 OCTOBER 1986.

'We have to alter our views on measures connected to the latest hostile behaviour by the American administration. The turn of events since Reykjavik reveals that our "friends" in the United States lack any positive programme and are doing everything to increase pressure on us.'

MIKHAIL GORBACHEV AT A POLITBURO MEETING, 22 OCTOBER 1986.

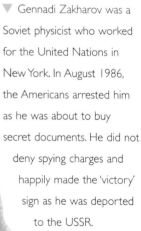

▼ Gennadi Zakharov was a Soviet physicist who worked for the United Nations in New York. In August 1986, the Americans arrested him as he was about to buy secret documents. He did not deny spying charges and happily made the 'victory' sign as he was deported to the USSR.

KEEP TALKING

Despite his anger at American behaviour in Reykjavik, Gorbachev knew that he had no choice but to return to the negotiating table. Without an end to the arms race, his reforms at home could not succeed. President Reagan, too, was eager to make progress. He needed to show the public some results, and to cut arms spending, which had made a huge dent in the government budget. So in 1987 both sides breathed new life into the arms reduction talks process. Their efforts led to an important breakthrough at the Washington summit in December.

PROGRESS ON INF

Gorbachev made the first move by declaring, in February 1987, that he was ready to go ahead with the zero option on intermediate-range nuclear forces (INF) even if the Americans refused to budge on SDI. American and Soviet negotiating teams then began to work out the detail of the agreement so that it could be signed later in the year. Soviet Foreign Minister Eduard Shevardnadze and US Secretary of State George Shultz also met regularly in an effort to solve particularly difficult problems. These included the highly sensitive issue of how each side could check that the other had destroyed its weapons.

BRITAIN AND FRANCE

The USA was not the only nuclear power in the West. Britain and France each had a nuclear capability whose missiles were not covered by Gorbachev's INF proposal. When British Prime Minister Margaret Thatcher visited Moscow in March 1987, the Soviet leader tried to convince her that the elimination of all nuclear weapons was vital. The 'Iron Lady' dismissed this idea. French President François Mitterrand shared her view. Fearing that Reagan would return to his 1986 plan of destroying all US nuclear weapons, both nations were particularly keen to maintain their independent nuclear deterrents.

THE WASHINGTON SUMMIT

The Washington summit, the third between Reagan and Gorbachev, began on 7 November 1987. The two leaders signed the INF treaty the next day. In so doing, they set in motion the destruction of a complete class of weapons – 1566 Soviet and 846 American – and accepted comprehensive on-site inspections for the verification of the process.

The INF treaty was a major milestone on the road to nuclear disarmament. However, intermediate-range weapons made up only about 3 per cent of the superpowers' combined nuclear arsenals. Even after the triumph of the Washington summit, a solution to the greater problem of reducing strategic weapon numbers was still not in sight.

▲ On arrival in the USA in December 1987, Gorbachev made a speech to the American people. By the time he left, the country had taken both him and his wife Raisa (standing on Gorbachev's right) to their hearts.

GORBYMANIA

On 10 December, the last day of the Washington summit, Gorbachev and his wife Raisa were as usual making their way through the city streets by limousine. Noticing the crowds cheering his progress, the Soviet leader asked his driver to stop, then got out and began greeting the people with handshakes and hugs. This was an experience that pleased him greatly and that he never forgot – the citizens of the USSR were much less appreciative of his efforts to bring about change.

'Gorbymania' was evident not only on the streets – the Soviet leader was also fêted at grand dinners and acclaimed by the media. The prestigious American magazine *Time* chose him as 'Man of the Year'.

▲ Some 2,000 Soviet troops in about 300 armoured vehicles head for home through a barren Afghan landscape in August 1988.

CHANGE IN MOSCOW

'Quite possibly, we're beginning to take down the barriers of the post-war era; quite possibly, we are entering a new era in history, a time of lasting change in the Soviet Union. We will have to see.'

PRESIDENT REAGAN TALKING ABOUT THE MOSCOW SUMMIT, 3 JUNE 1988.

'The Americans did not accept our bold and entirely realistic plan… directed at… a decisive transition toward the creation on the continent of a situation of non-offensive structure of arms and armed forces at a considerably reduced level. I believe that a good opportunity has been missed to get things moving, lessening the danger of confrontation between the two most powerful alliances and thus embracing national security.'

MIKHAIL GORBACHEV COMMENTING ON THE AMERICAN REFUSAL TO ACCEPT HIS PROPOSAL FOR TROOP REDUCTIONS IN EUROPE AT THE MOSCOW SUMMIT.

EXIT FROM AFGHANISTAN

In 1986, Gorbachev had described the war in Afghanistan, already six years old, as a 'bleeding wound'. In February 1988, he finally announced his intention to withdraw Soviet troops. An agreement on the mechanics of the process was signed at Geneva in April, and by February 1989 it was completed. The conflict between the *mujaheddin* and the Afghan government, now headed by Najibullah Ahmadzai, raged on for many years afterwards. Some 20,000 Soviet soldiers had died in vain.

THE MOSCOW SUMMIT

The fourth and final Reagan-Gorbachev summit took place from 29 May to 2 June 1988 and was notable more for its dramatic setting in Moscow than its arms control achievements. There were no major items on the agenda, since American intransigence about SDI made further movement on strategic weapons unlikely. However, the two leaders were able to ratify the 1987 INF treaty. Gorbachev also proposed that NATO and the Warsaw Pact, the Communist military alliance founded in 1955, should each cut back their conventional forces in Europe by half a million. The Americans were not ready to make such a huge gesture and rejected this idea.

The summit was, however, highly successful as a public relations exercise. On one occasion, Reagan and Gorbachev strolled around Red Square like old friends, providing the ideal photo-opportunity. When a journalist asked Reagan if he still thought the USSR was an evil empire, as he had in 1983, the answer was a firm 'No'. There could have been no clearer sign that the Cold War was fading fast.

NEW BEGINNINGS

In November, Republican George Bush was elected US President and prepared to take office in January. On 7 December, before he could do so, Gorbachev made a dramatic speech at the United Nations. Over the next two years, he announced, the USSR would cut its forces in Europe by half a million men, 10,000 tanks, 8,500 pieces of artillery and 800 aircraft. This would happen whether the USA reduced its forces or not. Gorbachev also stressed his commitment to 'freedom of choice', implying that lands in Eastern Europe should be able to govern themselves as they chose.

The Americans were delighted with this development and Reagan bade his Soviet counterpart a fond farewell at the end of the meeting. However, many high-ranking members of the Soviet military were appalled at the cuts in conventional arms. In the future, more and more of Gorbachev's problems were to come from among his own people.

▷ Gorbachev makes his ground-breaking speech about Soviet military cutbacks at the United Nations, New York in December 1988.

HUMAN RIGHTS

By 1988, the progress that the USSR had made on human rights issues was also clear. Gorbachev had abandoned Soviet Communism's long-standing persecution of religious organizations. So in June, the Russian Orthodox Church was able to celebrate publicly the 1000th anniversary of its foundation. The two most famous Soviet dissidents had already been released, in 1986. Anatoly Sharansky, a Jew who had monitored the USSR's breaches of the Helsinki Final Act, was allowed to emigrate to Israel. Andrei Sakharov, a physicist and human rights campaigner, was released from internal exile in the city of Gorky. In 1989, he became a member of the new Congress of People's Deputies, but died shortly afterwards.

41

CHAPTER SIX

The Final Years

WHITE HOUSE CAUTION

Once he had taken office in 1989, US President George Bush put the brakes on the arms reduction process. He wanted to make his own assessment of the Soviets, so ordered a wide-ranging review of US-Soviet relations. Its conclusion was that the USSR could not yet be trusted. Yes, Gorbachev had made progress on arms control and domestic policy. But was he just strengthening the Soviet economy before reviving the nuclear threat? And who could guarantee he would not be replaced by a more aggressive leader? Bush decided to watch and wait – the USA would be making no new arms concessions for the foreseeable future.

MOVING TOO SLOW?

'[I'm] sick and tired of getting beat up day after day for having no vision and letting Gorbachev run the show. This is not just public relations we are involved in. There's real danger in jumping ahead. Can't people see that?'

GEORGE BUSH REACTING TO COMPLAINTS THAT HE WAS TOO SLOW TO RESPOND TO GORBACHEV'S ARMS REDUCTION PLANS.

BUILDING BRIDGES

As time passed, the Bush team nevertheless began to work more closely with the Soviets. Secretary of State James Baker and Eduard Shevardnadze in particular developed a strong relationship. In May, the two met in Moscow and Baker saw for himself the chaos into which the USSR was sinking. It did not look like a country capable of launching a bid for world

▶ Bush's Secretary of State James Baker (left) and Soviet Foreign Minister Eduard Shevardnadze met for discussions in Moscow in May 1989.

domination. Gorbachev's announcement the same month that he was to remove 500 more warheads from Europe added to this impression.

EASTERN EUROPE

In the USSR and Eastern Europe, meanwhile, the situation was changing at breakneck speed. With his reforms, and his 1988 speech on 'freedom of choice', Gorbachev had unleashed forces that he simply could not control. Some Eastern European countries were beginning to dismantle their old, Soviet-controlled governments. Hungary was the first to make a move. In January 1989, its parliament legalized the formation of opposition parties and announced that democratic elections would take place in 1990. In May, the border with non-Communist Austria was opened and people began to move freely between the two nations.

There was change in Poland, too. An accord of April 1989 re-legalized the Solidarity union and permitted opposition parties. In the June elections that followed, Solidarity won the overwhelming majority of votes.

GEORGE HERBERT WALKER BUSH (1924-)

George Bush was born in Connecticut, the American state for which his father was a senator. He served as a navy pilot in the Second World War, then took an economics degree at Yale University. After graduating, he moved to Texas to set up an oil-drilling business.

Bush's political career began in 1966, and he was elected to the House of Representatives as a Republican the following year. In 1970, he became US ambassador to the United Nations, then, after a brief spell as chairman of the Republican Party National Committee, was sent to China as President Ford's special envoy. In 1976, after he had returned to the USA, Bush took over as head of the CIA, but was replaced when President Carter took office in 1977. He became Reagan's Vice President in 1981.

Bush successfully ran for President himself in 1988, winning widespread support by proclaiming: 'Read my lips – no new taxes.' As President, his major achievements included the continuation of the dialogue with the USSR that led to the end of the Cold War, and leadership of the 1991 Gulf War campaign against Iraq. George Bush lost the 1992 presidential election to Democrat Bill Clinton.

CHANGE IN CHINA

Since 1985, Gorbachev had tried to reduce tensions between the USSR and China. Finally, in May 1989, he set out for Beijing to normalize relations between the two countries. While there, he witnessed a huge, anti-government demonstration in the city's Tiananmen Square. The day after he left, the crowds were brutally dispersed by troops. It was not only in the USSR and Europe that Communism was under pressure.

ALL CHANGE

The relationship between the American and Soviet governments slowly improved in the second half of 1989. Meanwhile, the pace of change in Eastern Europe grew ever faster. One by one, countries that had been under the Soviet thumb for over 40 years threw off Communist rule.

CHANGING VIEWS

In July 1989, George Bush went to Poland and Hungary to see for himself the momentous events happening there. The real sense of enthusiasm for democracy moved the President, and he began to reconsider his views about Gorbachev. After the trip, he wrote to the Soviet leader proposing that they meet. It was eventually agreed that a summit would take place off Malta later in the year.

Before the summit, Soviet Foreign Minister Eduard Shevardnadze visited James Baker for talks at his Wyoming ranch. A breakthrough came when Shevardnadze announced the USSR would continue START talks without any American concession on SDI.

CONTROL OF EASTERN EUROPE

'We're not here to make you choose between East and West… we're not here to poke a stick in the eye of Mr Gorbachev; just the opposite – [we're here] to encourage the very kind of reforms that he is championing…'

EXTRACT FROM A SPEECH MADE BY PRESIDENT GEORGE BUSH DURING HIS VISIT TO POLAND IN JULY 1989. AS COMMUNISM WAS FADING IN EASTERN EUROPE, HE COULD HAVE CHOSEN TO CHALLENGE SOVIET POWER THERE. INSTEAD, BY THIS TIME, HE HAD DECIDED TO BACK GORBACHEV.

'Any interference in domestic affairs of any kind, any attempts to limit the sovereignty of states… is impermissible.'

EXTRACT FROM A SPEECH MADE BY GORBACHEV TO THE COUNCIL OF EUROPE ON 6 JULY 1989. THE WORDS CLEARLY CONTRADICT THE EARLIER BREZHNEV DOCTRINE, AND SO MARK ANOTHER IMPORTANT TURNING POINT.

THE FALL OF THE WALL

Gorbachev was busy elsewhere. In early October, he visited the German Democratic Republic (East Germany), a country celebrating the 40th anniversary of its formation, which occurred when Germany was divided into Communist East and democratic West in 1949. East Germany was led by Erich Honecker, a hard-line Communist with little patience for Gorbachev or his reforms. His people, however, were eager for change, as well as for reunification with West Germany.

Gorbachev's visit fuelled unrest and after he left on 7 October, mass protests

began. Honecker was ousted by security chief Egon Krenz, who introduced some reforms, but could not resist the pressure for further change. So on 9 November, the government announced that the Berlin Wall, which had divided the city between East and West since 1961, would open that night. Thousands gathered to make their way joyfully through the crossing points. Others dismantled the concrete structure, reducing much of this hated Cold War symbol to rubble.

▲ Lifting equipment removes part of the Berlin Wall as crowds watch. From the time the wall was erected in 1961 until its fall in 1989, at least 80 people were shot dead trying to escape across it from East to West.

BULGARIA AND CZECHOSLOVAKIA

Unrest soon spread: in November Bulgaria's Communist leader, Todor Zhivkov, was overthrown. Then the non-violent 'Velvet Revolution' began in Czechoslovakia. After mass protests in Prague, the country's Communist leader, Milos Jakes, resigned on 24 November. Within a week, the constitution was amended to deprive the Communist Party of its 'leading role'.

Further protests led to democratic elections in December. Alexander Dubcek, a long-standing opponent of the Communist regime, became federal assembly chairman. Playwright Vaclav Havel, who had played a major role in the reform movement, became President.

▼ Soon-to-be President Vaclav Havel waves to ecstatic crowds gathered in Prague, the capital of Czechoslovakia, in December 1989. They are celebrating the establishment of a democratically elected government.

THE MALTA SUMMIT

Gorbachev had met Bush when he was still US Vice President. But the two-day talks held on ships off the coast of Malta in December 1989 were the first occasion when both men sat down together as heads of state. By the time they did so, Bush was broadly convinced of Soviet good intentions and ready to deal. Gorbachev, struggling to cope with unrest in Eastern Europe and at home, was even more keen to make progress.

THE END OF THE COLD WAR

'We buried the Cold War at the bottom of the Mediterranean Sea.'

AN ASSESSMENT OF THE MALTA SUMMIT BY SOVIET FOREIGN MINISTRY SPOKESMAN GENNADY GERASIMOV.

ARMS AGENDA

Both leaders wanted to move ahead with START and agreed their teams should prepare a treaty for the next summit. This was scheduled for mid-1990 in Washington. A second treaty, dealing with the reduction of conventional forces in Europe (CFE), was also to be produced for the same date.

Developments in Eastern Europe were another important area of discussion. Bush wanted assurances from Gorbachev that the USSR would not send in troops to revive the Communist regimes falling like dominoes across the region. The Soviet leader was more than happy to comply. The Brezhnev Doctrine was dead and buried.

▼ President Bush and Mikhail Gorbachev on board the Soviet ship *Maxim Gorky*, one of two vessels used for the Malta summit. The other was an American ship, USS *Belknap*.

Talks about Central America were less amicable. Bush made no effort to hide his anger at the continuing flow of Soviet arms to the region. He also blamed the USSR for not stopping its Communist ally, Cuba, from supplying the Sandinistas in Nicaragua. In response, Gorbachev said Cuban leader Fidel Castro did as he pleased, so Bush should complain to him directly. In any case, Gorbachev argued, the USA often intervened elsewhere, so could not criticize others for doing the same.

REBELLION IN ROMANIA

At the end of December 1989, another Communist regime was toppled in Eastern Europe. The dictator of Romania, Nicolae Ceausescu, had ruled with considerable brutality since 1956. However, he finally pushed his people too far in 1989 by sending a dissident Protestant priest, Laszlo Tokes, into exile. Mass street protests began in mid-December, but seemed unlikely to produce any lasting change. Then, however, the army turned against Ceausescu, too. He and his wife Elena were tried and shot on Christmas Day.

ECONOMIC ISSUES

A wide range of economic issues was discussed at the Malta summit, too. The US President now believed in *perestroika* and wanted to do all that he could to support Gorbachev's implementation of the policy. So he offered to provide economic advisers who would help the Soviets make the transition to a market economy. He also proposed a new and much more favourable trading agreement between the USA and the USSR.

▼ Elena and Nicolae Ceausescu. In the years before his death, Nicolae terrified the Romanian people into obeying his will. A brutal secret police force, the *Securitate*, was always on call to punish dissenters.

▲ This map shows the borders of the USSR and the fifteen republics of which it was composed. All except the Baltic states are now more loosely allied in the Commonwealth of Independent States.

INTERNAL COLLAPSE

In 1945, British Prime Minister Winston Churchill had called the new divide between Communist and democratic Europe 'the Iron Curtain'. By 1990, it no longer existed and a major part of the Cold War conflict had died along with it. The USSR was now continuing the ideological struggle almost alone. However, as the new decade began, the survival not only of Soviet Communism, but also of the country itself came under threat, as many Soviet republics began to demand their independence.

THE SOVIET REPUBLICS

The USSR (Union of Soviet Socialist Republics) was made up of 15 states with populations of different nationalities. Russia was by far the most dominant – in 1987, 50 of the 55 ministers at national government level were Russians. Among the rest, some accepted Russian rule, while others, especially the Baltic states of Estonia, Latvia and Lithuania, longed to be free. As these states watched Eastern Europe cast off Russian dominance, they stepped up their own plans to do likewise.

ARMENIA AND AZERBAIJAN

The first major nationalist flare-up of 1990 occurred in the southern states of Armenia and Azerbaijan. The dispute was over Nagorny Karabakh, a territory that formed part of Muslim Azerbaijan, but was home to many Christian Armenians. Armenia, encouraged by Gorbachev's new policies, wanted both to win its independence from Moscow and to seize Nagorny Karabakh from Azerbaijan. In January 1990, a brutal civil war broke out between the two states, and Gorbachev was forced to send in troops.

THE BALTIC STATES

The Baltic states' clamour for freedom had begun in the 1980s, after Gorbachev came to power. Then, in March 1990, Lithuania declared its independence. The Soviet leader was not prepared to tolerate this move. He wanted to reform the Union, not to dissolve it. So, Gorbachev ordered troops to occupy government buildings in the Lithuanian capital, Vilnius, and blocked oil and gas supplies to the state. As a result, the independence declaration was temporarily suspended in July.

The two other Baltic states were undeterred. Estonia voted for its independence later in March 1990, and Latvia followed in May. However, like Lithuania, they were not yet able to implement their plans fully.

BORIS YELTSIN AND RUSSIA

Change was also under way in the Russian Republic. At the forefront of these developments was a reforming politician called Boris Yeltsin. Until he was sacked by Gorbachev in 1987, Yeltsin had been leader of the Communist Party in Moscow. By 1990, he was no longer a member of the Party at all, and preached a different doctrine from the Soviet leader. In his view, the USSR could not be saved, but would have to be dissolved. Yeltsin was appointed head of the Russian Republic by its new parliament on 29 May. The scene was set for a major clash of wills.

▼ Boris Yeltsin gains support on a visit to a collective farm near Moscow during an information tour on agriculture.

THE REUNIFICATION OF GERMANY

Since the fall of the Berlin Wall in November 1989, pressure for the reunification of Germany had been mounting. The Chancellor of West Germany, Helmut Kohl, was pushing especially hard for progress. However, the issue was complex and took many months to resolve.

TWO-PLUS-FOUR

The Soviets and the Western powers had different plans for Germany. Gorbachev, who had hoped to avoid reunification, wanted any new state to be neutral. The West wanted it to be a member of NATO and to side firmly with the rest of democratic Europe. So it was clear that detailed talks would be necessary before a united Germany could be achieved.

In February 1990, US Secretary of State James Baker suggested holding 'Two-plus-Four' talks that would include both Germanys plus the USSR, USA, Britain and France. These last four nations had jointly occupied Germany at the end of the Second World War, so had an interest in its future. The plan was accepted by all involved.

▼ President Gorbachev and West German Chancellor Helmut Kohl were already discussing Germany's future when they met in Bonn in June 1989, long before reunification in October 1990.

MAKING PROGRESS

Throughout the spring, the two Germanys worked on the detail of the reunification process – in May, for example, they signed a treaty introducing economic and monetary union. Gorbachev and Bush met from 30 May to 2 June in the USA, where the Soviet leader reluctantly accepted that the new Germany would join NATO. There were yet more talks in London, then Helmut Kohl went to the USSR to see Gorbachev.

The talks between the two men were crucial. Kohl managed to persuade the Soviet leader to abandon every last scrap of power over Germany, and in particular to withdraw all troops from the East. The Germans were delighted, but the hard-line Communists in Moscow were appalled. So, too, was Foreign Minister Eduard Shevardnadze, who was barely consulted, but still had to defend Gorbachev's decision.

Germany was finally reunited on 3 October 1990. Crowds gathered in Berlin to celebrate and Kohl proudly waved to his people. However, the two countries had been divided for 41 years, and the task of making them one nation again would continue long into the future.

TROUBLED TIMES

By late 1990, Gorbachev was in trouble. Nationalism was tearing the USSR apart, and he was being criticized by reformers and hard-liners alike. The Soviet leader now sided with the old-style Communists and introduced strict measures to control the population. In particular, he announced the army would fire on protesters if attacked. Shevardnadze resigned on 20 December, warning the USSR risked becoming a dictatorship.

THE CFE TREATY

At the Malta summit in 1989 the USA and the USSR had agreed to prepare a treaty that would limit conventional forces in Europe (CFE). This CFE treaty was eventually signed not only by the two superpowers but also by 20 other nations at a meeting held in Paris on 19 November 1990. It dealt with both troops and arms, and was another important sign of improving relations between East and West.

THE NEW GERMANY

'Whether we like it or not, the time will come when a united Germany will be in NATO, if that is its choice. Then, if that is its choice, to some degree and in some form, Germany can work together with the Soviet Union.'

MIKHAIL GORBACHEV SPEAKING AT A PRESS CONFERENCE DURING CHANCELLOR HELMUT KOHL'S VISIT TO THE USSR IN JULY 1990.

UNDER PRESSURE

In the early part of 1991, Gorbachev's problems worsened almost daily. The USSR was splintering as one republic after another made moves towards independence, while the country's economic decline was accelerating. Boris Yeltsin was taking every possible opportunity to stir up opposition to Gorbachev's rule. Everywhere he was under pressure.

THE GULF WAR

There were problems abroad, too. In August 1990, the Arab state of Iraq had invaded its smaller neighbour, Kuwait. The Americans had protested at once and begun to mass troops in nearby Saudi Arabia. The Soviets, however, were unsure which side to support. Should they back their new friend the USA, or their old ally Iraq? In the event they very publicly backed the USA.

Soviet support for the Americans included voting for a 1990 United Nations resolution on Kuwait. This stated that if the Iraqis had not left by 15 January 1991, it was permissible to eject them by force. The deadline duly arrived, but Iraq's leader, Saddam Hussein, ordered his troops to stay. The USA and its 27 allies therefore launched a series of aerial attacks, codenamed Operation Desert Storm. The alliance's military planners, meanwhile, prepared for a ground war to begin on 24 February.

Before the ground troops arrived, Gorbachev made a direct effort to patch up the quarrel between his old and new allies by holding talks with

▼ American troops in Kuwait City, the capital of Kuwait, on 27 February 1991. They are waving their national flag and making the victory sign to celebrate their speedy defeat of Iraqi troops in the Gulf War.

Tariq Aziz, the Iraqi Foreign Minister. Aziz was, however, immoveable, and the Allied invasion went ahead. In an operation of textbook precision, Iraq's forces were driven out in a matter of days.

DIFFICULT QUESTIONS

Back in the USSR, Gorbachev and Yeltsin were still slogging it out. Gorbachev was determined to win support for his idea of a reformed USSR. It should, he argued, still have a central government, but all its republics should also be sovereign and equal. On 17 March 1991, he held a referendum to see how much of the population agreed with him. It was a pleasing 76.4 per cent. Now all he had to do was draft a treaty that incorporated his plans, a task that he was never properly able to finish.

Gorbachev's pleasure at the referendum result was marred by the fact that Boris Yeltsin had insisted on posing a second question on the same paper. This was, quite simply, should Russia have its own President? The answer, by 70 to 30 per cent, was yes. Yeltsin himself was democratically elected to the new role on 12 June. Now he was in an even better position to challenge his rival. Gorbachev was President of the USSR, but he had not been elected by popular vote.

THE WARSAW PACT

The military alliance known as the Warsaw Pact, or more fully the Eastern European Mutual Assistance Pact, was founded in 1955. Its members were the USSR and its Eastern European satellites. Its purpose was to serve as a counterbalance to NATO, the Western defence organization established in 1949. In January 1991, Poland, Hungary and Czechoslovakia announced that, from July, they would no longer play any part in the organization. Bulgaria made the same declaration in February. On 31 March 1991, the alliance effectively ceased to exist and in July it was officially dissolved. Another Cold War symbol had gone.

THE END OF THE COLD WAR

By the summer of 1991, little remained of the Cold War conflict. But Mikhail Gorbachev, the man who had done most to bring about its end, was struggling to keep the USSR together. It was a lost cause.

G7

The ailing Soviet economy was among Gorbachev's major concerns. So he turned for help to G7, the group of the world's seven richest nations. At a meeting in London on 17 July 1991, Gorbachev presented them with a new economic plan for the USSR. They were not impressed. President Bush had already made clear that there was no question of American financial aid unless the country could show exactly how it intended to turn itself into a market economy. Gorbachev's plan did nothing of the sort so, to his anger, his appeal was rejected.

START I

▼ Holding Russian flags and photographs of the Russian President, Muscovites listen to Boris Yeltsin as he denounces the anti-Gorbachev coup of August 1991.

There was better news on arms reduction. Presidents Bush and Gorbachev signed the START I treaty in Moscow in July 1991. It restricted each of the superpowers to a maximum of 9,000 warheads and bombs, and 1,500 delivery vehicles (that is ICBMs, SLBMs and bomber aircraft). The plan was that further reductions would follow.

THE AUGUST COUP

Since June, there had been rumours that hard-line Communists were about to oust Gorbachev. On 19 August, while the Soviet leader was away from Moscow on holiday, the rebels struck. Tanks rolled into the streets of the capital, the radio and television networks were seized and a state of emergency was imposed. Gennady Yanayev, Gorbachev's Vice President and one of the plotters, took over as leader.

Boris Yeltsin now took the step that was to seal his victory over Gorbachev. Standing on top of a tank outside the White House, the Russian parliament building, he declared to the crowds below that the coup was unconstitutional and should be resisted. This was enough to turn the tide firmly against the half-hearted and hesitant leaders of the rebellion. On 22 August, Gorbachev was able to return from his holiday home on the Black Sea coast. But Yeltsin was now in control.

▲ The people shown on page 54 were looking at a scene like this outside the Russian White House. Yeltsin, the man standing on a tank at its centre, was officially criticizing Mikhail Gorbachev's hard-line opponents. But he had his own dreams of power, too.

FROM USSR TO CIS

The failed coup put an end to Gorbachev's dreams of a revived USSR. Realizing how weak the Union really was, the Baltic states and other republics finally broke free. On 24 August Gorbachev resigned as General Secretary of the Soviet Communist Party. Five days later, the operations of the Party itself were suspended.

Now everything was in limbo. All the individual republics still existed but it was unclear how, or if, they should relate to one another. This problem was solved by Boris Yeltsin, the Russian leader, along with the leaders of two newly independent republics, Belarus and Ukraine. On 8 December, they met in Minsk, the capital of Belarus, and formally dissolved the USSR. Then, they set up the Commonwealth of Independent States (CIS), a much looser association of republics that was quickly joined by nine others. The three Baltic states, however, chose to remain completely independent.

AN UNCERTAIN END

Gorbachev officially resigned as President of the USSR on 25 December 1991 with a poignant speech. Then the Soviet hammer and sickle flag was lowered over the Kremlin for the last time and replaced with the red, white and blue tricolour of Russia. A once mighty country was dead and the Cold War was over. No one knew what would follow.

THE VANISHING ENEMY

'We have seen our implacable enemy of 40 years vaporize before our eyes.'

GENERAL COLIN POWELL, THEN CHAIRMAN OF THE AMERICAN JOINT CHIEFS OF STAFF, 27 SEPTEMBER 1991.

CHAPTER SEVEN

The Cold War Legacy

The Vietnam Veterans' Memorial in Washington D.C. is carved with the names of Americans killed or missing in Vietnam. Throughout the year, especially on Vietnam Veterans' Memorial Day (29 May), people make rubbings of lost friends' and relatives' names to take home.

THE WHOLE WORLD was in the grip of the Cold War for 45 years. Some countries participated directly, others only at a distance, but the possibility of a nuclear holocaust hung over all. The legacy of conflict on such a scale is inevitably both wide-ranging and enduring.

THE USA

In so far as the Cold War had a winner, it was the USA. As the self-styled champion of democracy, it had triumphed over Communism. As a superpower, it had effectively eliminated its only rival. The country was also quickly able to bounce back from the budget deficits caused by high military spending ($400 billion per year in the Reagan era, for example). However, at a personal level, the Cold War left a far more tragic legacy. Some 54,000 US troops died in the Korean War and almost 58,000 in Vietnam. Many thousands more were wounded.

THE USSR AND RUSSIA

The USSR was a clear loser – so much so that it ceased to exist. The republics formed from its remains are still struggling to recover.

Under Boris Yeltsin, then Vladimir Putin, his successor from December 1999, Russia has faced particular problems. The economy has steadily declined, and many people are not paid for months. This includes members of the armed forces. The state cannot even afford to maintain its nuclear installations and weapons. Crime has also risen dramatically, as the Russian Mafia exploits the country's weakness.

NUCLEAR DISARMAMENT

In the immediate aftermath of the Cold War, the USA and Yeltsin's Russia continued to co-operate on arms reduction. As a result, they were able to sign START II in 1993. When introduced, it will limit each side to 3,500 nuclear weapons each. All land missiles with multiple warheads will be eliminated. However, the breakdown of law and order in Russia is so great that it is hard to keep track of the country's nuclear weapons.

EASTERN EUROPE

Many Eastern European countries have flourished since gaining their independence, becoming politically and economically stable. In 1994, NATO launched a 'partnership for peace' that encouraged these nations to co-operate militarily with the West. Some, including Poland, have since joined the alliance, and the hope is that Europe will become more secure as a result. Several Eastern European countries have also applied to join the European Union.

GERMANY

Like Russia, Germany has had to cope with particular difficulties following the end of the Cold War. Reunification led to severe economic problems, including high unemployment, which reached 4.27 million in 1996. There has also been a growth in racism and neo-Nazi activity directed against Turkish and other immigrant workers in the East.

▲ Vladimir Putin, Boris Yeltsin's successor as President of Russia. Before entering politics, Putin was an official in the KGB, the Soviet secret police, then head of the Federal Security Service, a similar Russian institution set up after the collapse of the USSR.

YUGOSLAVIA

Although not a Soviet satellite, the former Yugoslavia was a relatively stable Communist country until the death of its long-term ruler, Marshal Tito, in 1980. Then, gradually, Serbia, Croatia and the other republics of which it was composed began to split apart. This process led to a series of bloody civil wars fuelled by ethnic and religious hatreds, and, eventually, the fragmentation of the country.

Some historians and other experts argue that one of the few virtues of the Cold War stand-off was to prevent such situations from developing. According to this argument, fear of the main enemy and firm government stopped lesser conflicts from rising to the surface.

A CHANGING WORLD

In 1990, President George Bush said that he believed the end of the Cold War would lead to the creation of a 'new world order'. In fact, that has not, or at least not yet, become part of the Cold War legacy. There is no settled new global situation to replace the dependable rivalry of those years. Instead, many countries are struggling to find their place in the world under these new, unpredictable and often dangerous conditions.

CHINA

Since the collapse of the USSR, China has become the world's only major Communist power. Many experts believe that, with its own nuclear capability, a booming economy thanks to reforms introduced during the 1980s, and a huge population of well over 1 billion, the country will one day become a superpower equal to the USA.

CUBA, VIETNAM AND NORTH KOREA

The world's other remaining Communist nations are not flourishing. Cuba, still led by Fidel Castro, suffered greatly from the withdrawal of Soviet trade subsidies and troops in 1990. Vietnam felt the same loss, but in recent years has made efforts to draw closer to the USA. In 1994, the Americans lifted their embargo on trade with the country, and in 2000, US President Bill Clinton paid a visit there.

North Korea was virtually cut off from the rest of the world during the long and repressive dictatorship of Kim Il Sung. After his death in 1994, he was replaced by his son, Kim Jong Il, who continued similar policies. However, in 2000,

▼ The leader of Communist North Korea, Kim Jong Il (left), greets the President of non-Communist South Korea, Kim Dae Jung. This historic meeting took place in Pyongyang on 13 June 2000, 55 years after their country was split in two.

moves were made to improve relations with non-Communist South Korea. The countries' two leaders met in the North Korean capital, Pyongyang, and 100 people from each side of the border were allowed to cross it briefly to visit relatives.

WAR AND PEACE

The end of the Cold War has not removed the threat of 'hot' war. In 1992, there were 66 wars raging in various parts of the world. A similar number are still going on. The threat of nuclear war is not over either. The world's nuclear powers still own combined arsenals capable of exploding with 8 megatonnes of force.

Since January 2001, when new US President George W. Bush took office, Cold War tensions have re-emerged. In March, the USA expelled 50 Russian spies, and Russia the same number of Americans. Then, on 1 April, an American spy plane collided with a Chinese fighter plane off the coast of China's Hainan Island and made an emergency landing. When China refused to release the plane and its 24 crew immediately, the relationship between the world's leading capitalist and Communist powers grew strained. More generally, Bush is preparing for the worst by planning to build a Star Wars-style National Missile Defence (NMD) system.

Despite these setbacks, the world is still a safer place than it was at the height of the Cold War. Thanks to patient years of arms talks, many missiles have been destroyed and the threat of nuclear disaster has faded into the background.

THE UNITED NATIONS

The work of the United Nations (UN), which was formed in 1945 to carry out peacekeeping and many other roles, was hampered by the Cold War. This was because each side in the conflict tried to prevent the other from having its way there. In particular the USA and USSR, which were both members of the Security Council, used their vetoes to block proposals that they did not like.

Since the end of the Cold War, the UN has become less divided, and has also increased its peacekeeping role, sending troops to areas such as the former Yugoslavia, the Middle East, El Salvador and Angola. However, there are still restrictions on its work that can make it ineffective. UN soldiers keep the peace, they do not make it, so cannot intervene to prevent fighting. Their job is mainly to observe and mediate in disputes without using force.

COLD WAR STABILITY

'For all its risk and uncertainties, the Cold War was characterized by a remarkably stable and predictable set of relationships among the great powers.'

LAWRENCE EAGLEBURGER, DEPUTY US SECRETARY OF STATE,
SEPTEMBER 1989.

Timeline

1972

22 FEBRUARY
US President Richard
Nixon visits China

26 MAY
USA and USSR sign
SALT I treaty in Moscow

1973

27 JANUARY
USA signs Vietnam
War truce in Paris

1974

8 AUGUST
US President Nixon
resigns; Gerald Ford
takes over

1980

23 JANUARY
US President Carter
proclaims the Carter
Doctrine in his State of
the Union speech

17 SEPTEMBER
Solidarity (Solidarnosc)
trade union founded
in Poland

1981

13 DECEMBER
Polish Prime Minister
Jaruzelski declares
martial law

1982

12 NOVEMBER
Yuri Andropov becomes
General Secretary of the
Soviet Communist Party
following the death of
Leonid Brezhnev

19-21 NOVEMBER
First Reagan-Gorbachev
summit meeting held in
Geneva, Switzerland

1986

10-12 OCTOBER
Second Reagan-
Gorbachev summit
meeting held in
Reykjavik, Iceland

1987

7-10 DECEMBER
Third Reagan-
Gorbachev summit
meeting held in
Washington DC; INF
treaty signed on
second day

1990

9 NOVEMBER
The Berlin Wall opens,
allowing people to pass
freely between the East
and West of the city;
much of the wall is
pulled down

2-3 DECEMBER
First Bush-Gorbachev
summit held off the
coast of Malta

29 MAY
Boris Yeltsin appointed
leader of the Russian
Republic

30 MAY – 2 JUNE
Second Bush-
Gorbachev summit held

in Washington DC

2 AUGUST
Iraq invades Kuwait

3 OCTOBER
East and West Germany
reunited

1975

24 NOVEMBER
Vladivostok Accord
agreed between
President Ford and
General Secretary of
the Soviet Communist
Party, Leonid Brezhnev

1 AUGUST
Helsinki Final
Act signed

1979

18 JUNE
USA and USSR sign
SALT II treaty in Vienna

12 DECEMBER
NATO countries approve
deployment of new
cruise and Pershing II

ballistic missiles
in Europe.

25 DECEMBER
Red Army invades
Afghanistan

1983

23 MARCH
President Reagan
launches the Strategic
Defense Initiative
('Star Wars')

23 NOVEMBER
Soviets walk out of the
START and INF talks
in Geneva

1984

13 FEBRUARY
Konstantin Chernenko
becomes General
Secretary of the Soviet
Communist Party
following death of
Yuri Andropov

1985

11 MARCH
Mikhail Gorbachev
becomes General
Secretary of the Soviet
Communist Party
following death of
Konstantin Chernenko

1988

29 MAY-2 JUNE
Fourth and final
Reagan-Gorbachev
summit held in
Moscow, USSR

7 DECEMBER
Gorbachev announces
huge Soviet arms cuts
and commitment to
'freedom of choice' in
Eastern Europe

1989

15 FEBRUARY
Last Soviet troops
leave Afghanistan

15-19 MAY
Gorbachev visits Beijing
and normalizes

relations between
USSR and China;
pro-democracy
demonstration takes
place in Tiananmen
Square

1991

15 JANUARY
Operation Desert Storm
against Iraq begins

12 JUNE
Boris Yeltsin elected
President of the
Russian Republic

31 JULY
Bush and Gorbachev
sign the START I
treaty in Moscow

19 AUGUST
Gorbachev is
temporarily ousted by
hard-line Communist
rebels

8 DECEMBER
USSR is dissolved and
CIS established

25 DECEMBER
Gorbachev resigns as
President of the USSR

Glossary

Anti-ballistic missile A missile to intercept and destroy ballistic missiles.

Artillery The collective name for cannon and other types of heavy gun that have barrels with an interior diameter (calibre) of over 20mm.

Ballistic missile A missile without fins that continues towards its target even after its rocket motor has burned out. The force of gravity and the momentum already provided by the motor enable it to do so.

Colony A country or other territory that is occupied and ruled by another state.

Council of Europe An organization founded in 1949 to promote unity, democracy, economic progress and human rights in Europe. Most European states are members.

Counter-revolution A revolution that aims to overthrow the government established by a previous revolution.

Cruise missile A low-flying missile that, unlike a ballistic missile, is rocket-powered throughout its flight.

De facto Existing in fact, even if not legally or officially recognized.

Détente The process or policy of reducing tension between countries. (The word is French for 'loosening'.)

Dissident A person who opposes and acts against a government or other official body.

Gross national product The total value of all the goods and services that a country produces each year.

Internal exile Banishment to a place that is not one's home, but that is within the same country.

Market economy An economic system that is not strictly controlled by central government (a command economy), but that is free to supply goods and services in response to consumer demand.

Martial law Law imposed and enforced by armed forces, for example during times of national emergency.

Nationalist Chinese The party that governed China after imperial rule ended in 1911. In 1949, they lost a civil war against the Chinese Communists and fled to the island of Taiwan, which they still rule.

Politburo The main policy-making committee of the Soviet and many other Communist Parties. The word is a short form of the Russian for 'political bureau'.

Rapprochement The re-establishment of friendly relations between previously hostile countries. The word is French for 'drawing closer'.

Ratify To approve officially.

Satellite A country that is controlled by another, more powerful, state.

Secretary of State The American government minister who is in charge of foreign affairs.

Security Council The most powerful body in the United Nations. Its five permanent members (China, France, Russia, the United Kingdom and the USA) can veto any decision.

Sovereign state An independent state; one that is free to govern itself without outside intervention.

Strategic arms Large, long-range missiles capable of reaching targets up to 5,500 km (3,400 miles) away.

Further Information

BOOKS

Michael R. Beschloss and Strobe Talbott
At the Highest Levels: The Inside Story of the End of the Cold War
(Little, Brown, 1993)
A detailed account of the final years of the Cold War, including many quotations that give an insight into the minds of the main players.

Jeremy Isaacs and Taylor Downing
Cold War (Bantam Press, a division of Transworld Publishers Ltd, 1998)
A wide-ranging title written to accompany the CNN/BBC 2 TV series of the same name. Chapters 14 to 20 are particularly relevant to this book.

Mikhail Gorbachev
Memoirs (Doubleday, 1996)
The Soviet leader gives his own account of his years in power, his reforms and the collapse of both the USSR and the Cold War.

Lou Cannon *President Reagan, The Role of a Lifetime* (Simon and Schuster, 1991)
A biography of the American president who played such a major role in bringing the Cold War to an end.

WEBSITES

The USSR and Eastern Europe
1989-1991
A US site compiled by the Center for the Study of Intelligence. Contains articles about a range of events from these years, plus useful chronologies and downloadable CIA papers.
**http://www.odci.gov/csi/books/19335/
/art-1.html**

The Cold War
A wide-ranging site designed to accompany the CNN/BBC 2 TV series of the same name. The episodes relevant to this book are 16-24. To locate them, simply add /episodes/16 (17 etc.) to the end of the main web address below.
**http://www.cnn.com/SPECIALS/cold.
war**

The Cold War Museum
A US site featuring articles on a wide range of Cold War subjects divided by decade, a photo gallery, a discussion forum and much more.
http://www.coldwar.org

Gorbachev and Reagan
Profiles of these two important leaders from the USA's prestigious *Time* magazine. Brief chronologies are also included.
**http://www.time.com/time/time100/
leaders/profile/gorbachev.html**
**http://www.time.com/time/time100/
leaders/profile/reagan.html**

Visit learn.co.uk for more resources

Index